DAVID LANZ

new age piano selections from
bridge of dreams

contents:

"I always hope that my music will somehow, in some way, help people," says David Lanz. "Even if all it does is just get them to tap their toes, or smile a little or pause to think about things a little more deeply, I feel I'm making a positive contribution to someone's life."

Lanz, one of contemporary music's most popular pianists, pursues that ambition on BRIDGE OF DREAMS, an album he created in collaboration with guitarist and long-time friend Paul Speer.

"Musically, it's a statement about where I have been and where I am at the moment," says Lanz. "It's also a statement about where the world is today, and where we would all like to see it go."

Lanz based the music thematically around a short story that he authored. It follows the fictional experiences of a 10-year-old boy who lives in a grim, cheerless world that, following a night when everyone dreams the identical dream, is finally transformed by the music and singing of children.

"My personal vision is much wider and larger than I'm able to convey on an album of music," Lanz says, smiling. "This album provides one part of the story, a musical allegory of trusting in your true self. I am convinced that if we keep working to positively influence our lives from the inside out, we can brighten the world."

Cover photograph by Rosanne Olson
Design by Denyse Gattorna, Connie Gage, Eric Lindert and Wesley Van Linda

NP-90009SB
ISBN 0-7935-2929-8

Hal Leonard Publishing Corporation
7777 West Bluemound Road P.O. Box 13819 Milwaukee, WI 53213

Bridge of Dreams

By DAVID LANZ

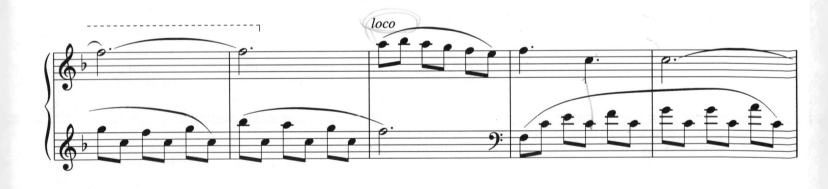

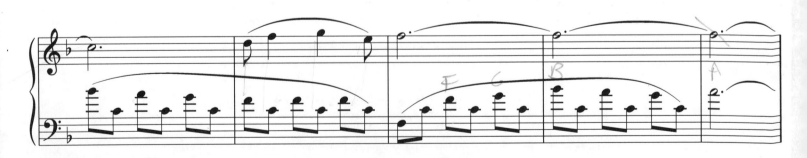

A Day in the Life

Composed by JOHN LENNON
and PAUL McCARTNEY
Arranged by DAVID LANZ

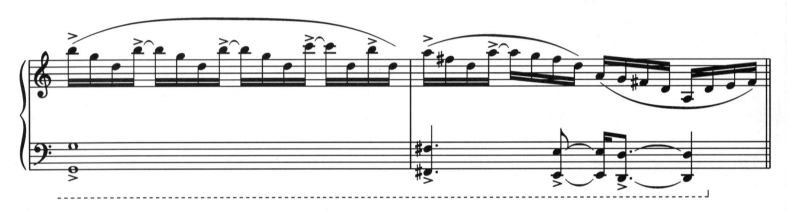

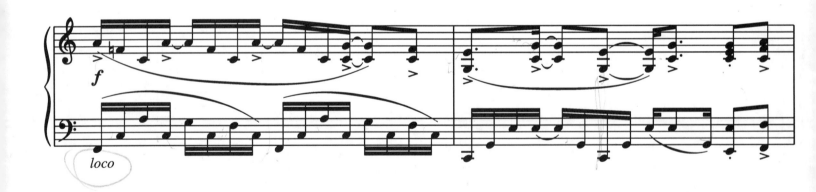

MCA music publishing

Into the Dream

By DAVID LANZ

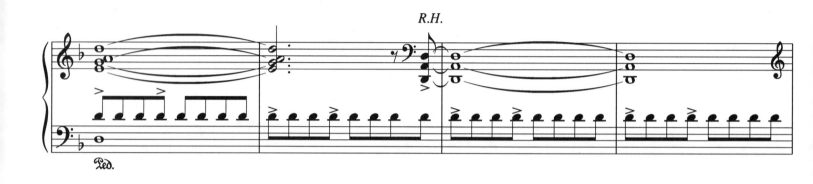

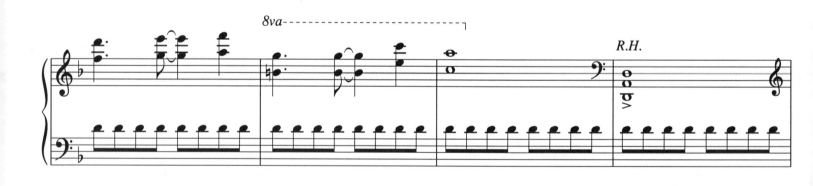

Ode to a Dark Star

By DAVID LANZ

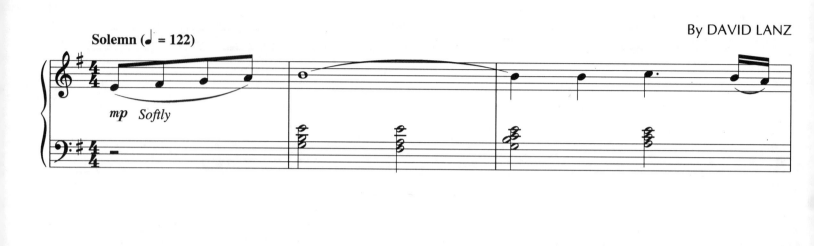

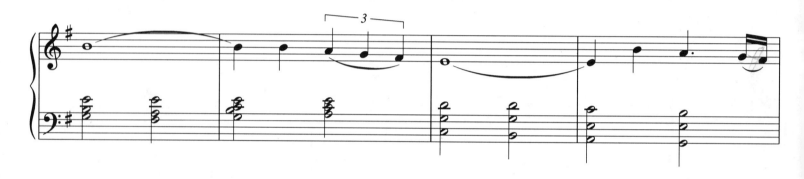

To Coda ⊕

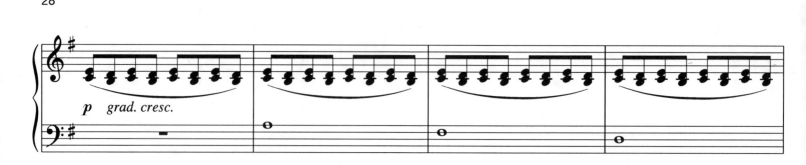

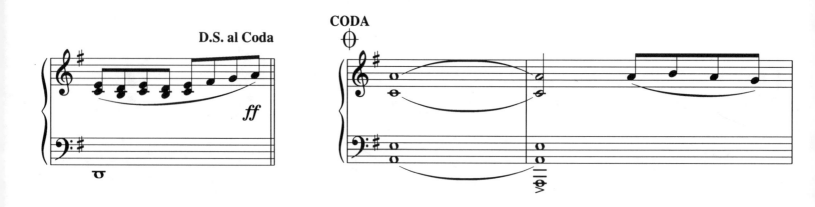

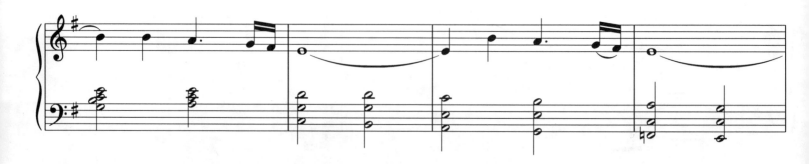

She Stands on the Mountain, Still

By DAVID LANZ

Moderately bright (♩ = 116)

8va bassa

mp

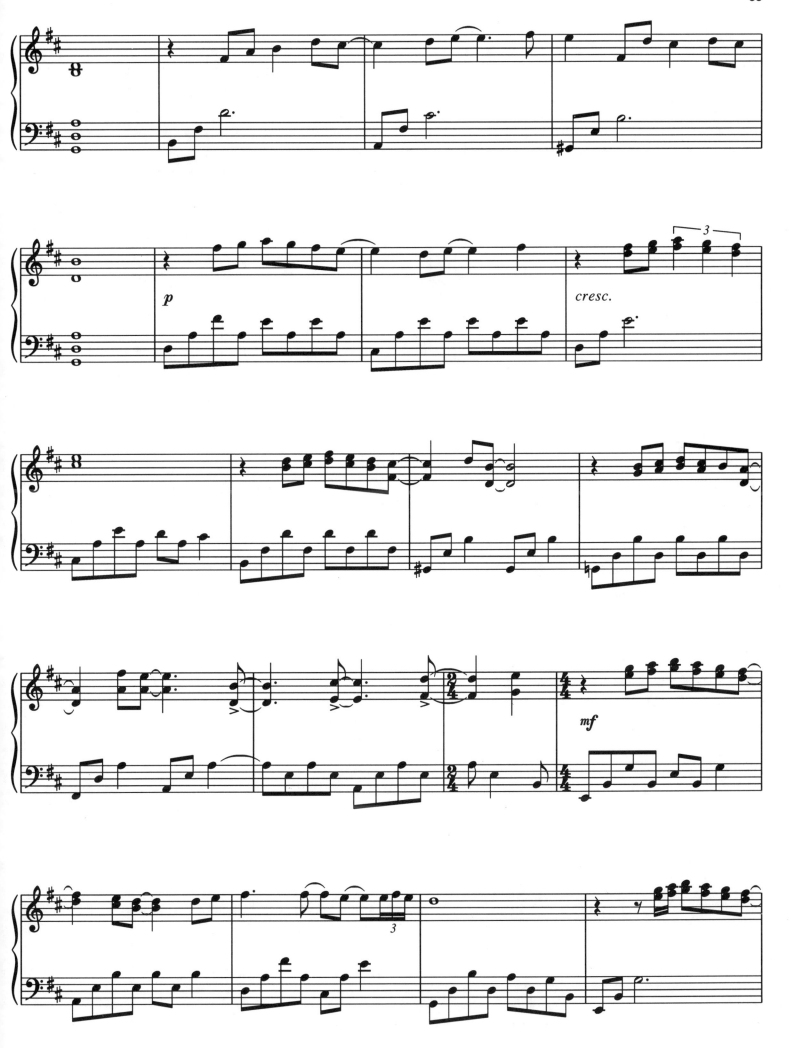

loco

8va bassa

pp

Song of the East
(In this Dream)

Words and Music
By DAVID LANZ

We are one, we are free to be-

Reverie

By DAVID LANZ

* Brightly (♩ = 118)

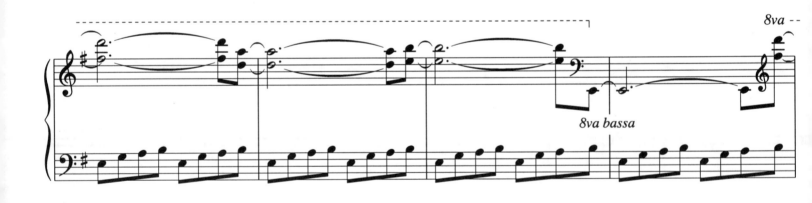

Original key of recording is E♭ minor.

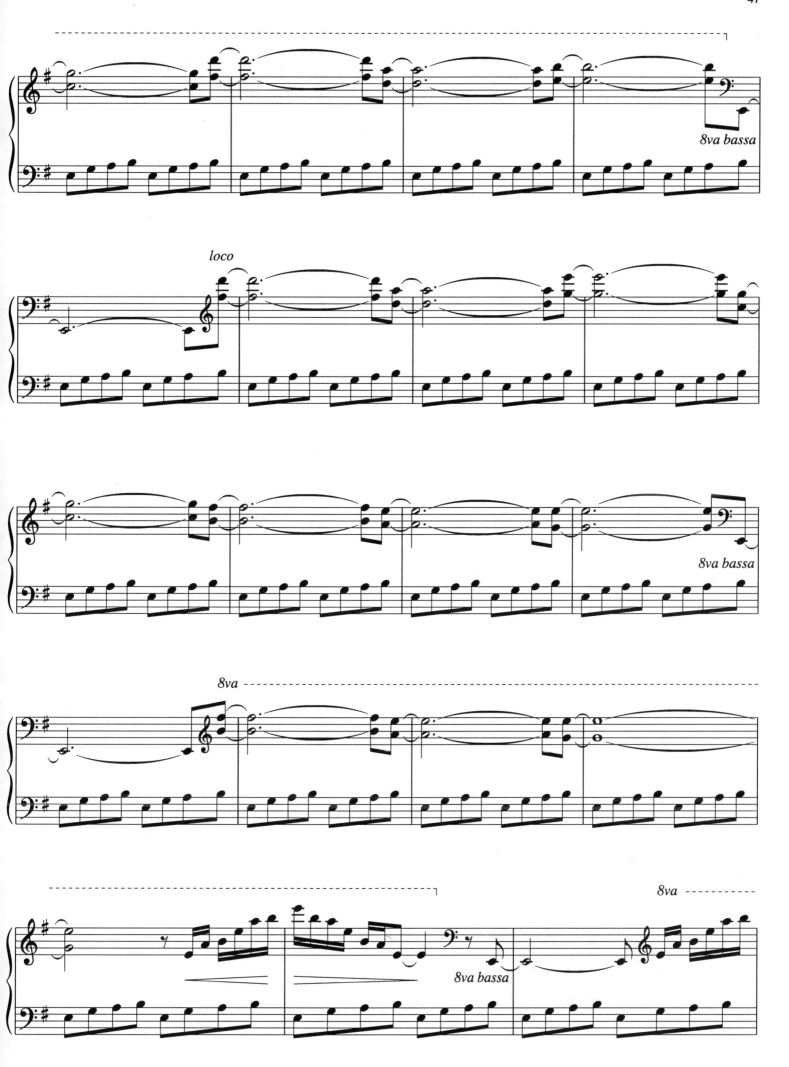

Veil of Tears

By DAVID LANZ

Whispered in Signs

Words and Music by
DAVID LANZ

Listen to the sound, the sound of si-lence roar-ing. You can hear it in the waves, I

know your heart re-mem-bers ev-'ry-thing it needs to know. A-wak-ened from its slum-ber. Ev-'ry-

thing it needs to know right now.

Lis-ten to the sound, the

out on the shore.

mp

Lis - ten to the sound, the

8va bassa -

a catalog of
narada recordings

NARADA LOTUS™
New Acoustic Music

N-61001 PIANOSCAPES Michael Jones
N-61002 SEASONS Gabriel Lee
N-61003 HEARTSOUNDS David Lanz
N-61004 SEASCAPES Michael Jones
N-61005 IMPRESSIONS Gabriel Lee
N-61006 NIGHTFALL David Lanz
N-61007 SAMPLER #1 Narada Artists
N-61008 SOLSTICE Jones and Lanz
N-61009 SUNSCAPES Michael Jones
N-61010 OPENINGS William Ellwood
N-61011 EMERALD
        Tingstad, Rumbel and Lanz
N-61012 QUIET FIRE Ancient Future
N-61013 SAMPLER #2 Narada Artists
N-61014 AMBER Jones and Darling
N-61015 RENAISSANCE William Ellwood
N-61016 WOODLANDS
        Tingstad, Rumbel and Lanz
N-61017 PORTRAITS Spencer Brewer
N-61018 SAMPLER #3 Narada Artists
N-61019 DEPARTURES John Doan
N-61020 AFTER THE RAIN Michael Jones
N-61021 CRISTOFORI'S DREAM
        David Lanz
N-61022 LEGENDS Tingstad and Rumbel
N-61023 REMINISCENCE Wayne Gratz
N-61024 VISTA William Ellwood
N-61025 SAMPLER #4 Narada Artists
N-61026 HOMELAND Tingstad/Rumbel
N-61027 MAGICAL CHILD Michael Jones
N-61028 PANORAMA Wayne Gratz
N-61029 WISDOM OF THE WOOD
        Narada Artists
N-61030 MORNING IN MEDONTE
        Michael Jones
N-61031 PIANO SOLOS Narada Artists
N-61032 GUITAR WORKS Narada Artists
N-61033 CAROUSEL Ira Stein
N-61034 FOLLOW ME HOME Wayne Gratz
N-61035 ROMANTIC INTERLUDES
        Spencer Brewer
N-61036 GIVE AND TAKE Tingstad/Rumbel
N-61037 WIND AND REED Narada Artists
N-61038 TOUCHSTONE William Ellwood
N-61039 SIMON Simon Wynberg

NARADA MYSTIQUE™
New Electronic Music

N-62001 VALLEY IN THE CLOUDS
        David Arkenstone
N-62002 THE WAITING Peter Buffett

N-62003 HIDDEN PATHWAYS
        Bruce Mitchell
N-62004 ONE BY ONE Peter Buffett
N-62005 A VIEW FROM THE BRIDGE
        Carol Nethen
N-62006 INTRUDING ON A SILENCE
        Colin Chin
N-62007 DANCING ON THE EDGE
        Bruce Mitchell
N-62008 CITIZEN OF TIME
        David Arkenstone
N-62009 MYSTIQUE SAMPLER ONE
        Narada Artists
N-62010 WARM SOUND IN A GRAY FIELD
        Peter Maunu
N-62011 THE MESSENGER Jim Jacobsen
N-62012 LOST FRONTIER Peter Buffett
N-62013 YONNONDIO Peter Buffett

NARADA EQUINOX™
Crossover/Jazz/World

N-63001 NATURAL STATES Lanz/Speer
N-63002 INDIAN SUMMER Friedemann
N-63003 DESERT VISION Lanz/Speer
N-63004 EQUINOX SAMPLER ONE
        Narada Artists
N-63005 ISLAND Arkenstone with White
N-63006 CIRCLE Ralf Illenberger
N-63007 CROSS CURRENTS
        Richard Souther
N-63008 DORIAN'S LEGACY
        Spencer Brewer
N-63009 HEART & BEAT Ralf Illenberger
N-63010 MIL AMORES Doug Cameron
N-63011 MOON RUN Trapezoid
N-63012 CAFÉ DU SOLEIL Brian Mann
N-63013 WHITE LIGHT Martin Kolbe
N-63014 NEW LAND Bernardo Rubaja
N-63015 TWELVE TRIBES Richard Souther
N-63016 EQUINOX SAMPLER TWO
        Narada Artists
N-63017 AQUAMARINE Friedemann
N-63018 THE PIPER'S RHYTHM
        Spencer Brewer
N-63019 PLACES IN TIME Michael Gettel
N-63020 JOURNEY TO YOU Doug Cameron
N-63021 SOLEIL Ralf Illenberger
N-63022 RHYTHM HARVEST
        The Michael Pluznick Group
N-63023 ASIAN FUSION Ancient Future
N-63024 BRIDGE OF DREAMS Lanz/Speer
N-63025 SKYWATCHING Michael Gettel

NARADA COLLECTION SERIES™

N-39100 THE NARADA COLLECTION
        Narada Artists
N-39117 THE NARADA COLLECTION TWO
        Narada Artists
N-63902 THE NARADA CHRISTMAS
        COLLECTION Narada Artists
N-63904 THE NARADA NUTCRACKER
        Narada Artists
N-63905 THE NARADA WILDERNESS
        COLLECTION Narada Artists
N-63906 THE NARADA COLLECTION
        THREE Narada Artists
N-63907 A CHILDHOOD REMEMBERED
        Narada Artists
N-63908 ALMA DEL SUR Various Artists
N-63909 NARADA CHRISTMAS
        COLLECTION VOLUME
        Narada Artists
N-63910 NARADA COLLECTION 4
        Narada Artists
N-63911 NARADA DECADE
        Narada Artists
N-63912 CELTIC ODYSSEY
        Various Artists
N-63913 EARTH SONGS Narada Artists

NARADA ARTIST SERIES™

N-64001 SKYLINE FIREDANCE David Lanz
N-64002 MICHAEL'S MUSIC Michael Jones
N-64003 IN THE WAKE OF THE WIND
        David Arkenstone
N-64004 IN THE GARDEN Tingstad/Rumbel
N-64005 RETURN TO THE HEART
        David Lanz
N-64006 The SPIRIT OF OLYMPIA
        Arkenstone, Kostia, Lanz
N-64007 CHRONICLES
        David Arkenstone

NARADA CINEMA™

N-66001 MILLENNIUM: TRIBAL WISDOM
        AND THE MODERN WORLD
        Hans Zimmer
N-66002 COLUMBUS AND THE AGE OF
        DISCOVERY Sheldon Mirowitz
N-66003 SPACE AGE Jay Chattaway
N-66004 THE DINOSAURS! Peter Melnick
N-66005 SEAPOWER Michael Whalen

Narada appreciates the support of its listeners, and we welcome your comments about the music of our artists.
Narada publishes a free, semi-annual newsletter that features
personal interviews with Narada artists as well as information on new recordings.
You may receive future copies by writing to us and joining our growing, worldwide family of quality-minded listeners.

Please write to:
Friends of Narada, 1845 N. Farwell Ave., Milwaukee, WI 53202 USA, or
Friends of Narada, P.O. Box 2301, 1200 CH Hilversum, Netherlands.